이제혁 시집
The Collection of Poeams of Jae Hyuk Lee
한영대역판
Korean-English Translation

세 번의 기도

Three Prayers

미산彌山 **이 제 혁** 시집
Sumeru, Jae Hyuk LEE

다솜출판사

Greetings

I have reflected on the idea that pursuing goodness and cultivating beauty in life may be one of the most fulfilling endeavors.

Although I have not been immersed in the world of poetry for long, I wish to live my life with a pure heart, nurturing its beauty. This is because I hope that the soul of poetry will never become dull. In a life that flies like an arrow, it may be a duty to expand the scope of existence—from rigidity to flexibility—both as individuals and as a society.

Looking back on the traces of my life traveling with my wife, suddenly the thoughts that unfold through my struggles in the world of poetry gave me the deep urge to share them with my wife and family.

Spring has ripened and is now transitioning into a season of abundance. Just like the approaching season, I, too, wish to enter a rich and bountiful season of poetry.

I sincerely hope for the encouragement of many readers.

May, 2025
Jae Hyuk Lee

인사 말씀

　사람이 사는 동안 선善을 추구하여 미美를 가꾸어 나가는 것이 보람된 일이 아닐까 생각해 본다.
　시詩의 세계에 뛰어든 지 오래지 않아도 순수한 마음으로 한 생生을 아름답게 가꾸며 살고 싶다. 시詩의 영혼이 녹슬지 않기를 바라기 때문이다. 화살 같은 인생에서 개인으로부터 사회에 이르기까지 경직됨에서 유연함으로 삶의 폭을 넓혀야 하는 것이 하나의 의무가 될지도 모른다.

　아내와 여행하며 함께 들여다본 삶의 족적들, 시詩의 세계에서 고뇌하며 펼쳐지는 사고思考를 풀어, 아내와 가족에게 내놓고 싶은 충동이 내 마음을 흔들어 놓았다.

　봄이 무르익어 지금 풍성의 계절로 들어가고 있다. 다가오는 계절처럼 풍요로운 시詩의 계절로 들어가고 싶다.

　많은 독자분의 격려를 바란다.

2025년 5월
이 제 혁

Part 1 The Journey of Life

14 / Three Prayers
18 / A Joyful Journey Together
20 / Still, I Must Go
22 / The Heart That Sends Off
24 / A Long Journey
26 / Prayer and Answer
28 / Oceania Journey
32 / A Life Like an Arrow
34 / At the Terminus
36 / The Empty Journey
38 / Tears-soaked Bread
40 / The Spirit of the Indian
42 / To That Place
44 / Autumn Reflections
46 / The Swing
48 / Silver Elegy
50 / Serenade of November
52 / Footprints on the Snow
54 / The Disappearance of a Model
56 / Eyelids
58 / Feast

제1부 함께하는 기쁜 여행

15 / 세 번의 기도
19 / 함께하는 기쁜 여행
21 / 그래도 가야지
23 / 떠나보내는 마음
25 / 긴 여행
27 / 기도와 대답
29 / 오세니아 여정
33 / 화살 같은 인생
35 / 종점에서
37 / 허무한 여정
39 / 눈물 젖은 빵
41 / 인디언 정령精靈
43 / 그곳으로
45 / 가을 사념思念
47 / 그네
49 / 은빛 엘리지
51 / 11월의 세레나데
53 / 눈 위의 발자국
55 / 모델의 실종
57 / 눈꺼풀
59 / 향연

Part 2 The Nest

64 / A Quiet Countryside Sketch
66 / My Wife's Footprints
68 / Together
70 / Badminton Story
72 / When May Comes
74 / Chuseok Sketch
76 / Scent of My Father
78 / To My Son
80 / Aching Heart
82 / My Favorite Fruit
84 / Sweet Potatoes
86 / Daughter's Birthday
88 / Single-Line Fishing
90 / Nest
92 / Couple
94 / Sincerity
96 / Aspiration
98 / Protagonist
100 / Memories Like Waves
102 / With You
104 / A Mayfly's Prayer

제2부 둥지

65 / 고즈넉한 시골의 소묘
67 / 아내의 발자국
69 / 함께
71 / 배드민턴 이야기
73 / 5월이 오면
75 / 추석 소묘
77 / 아버지의 향내
79 / 아들에게
81 / 아픈 가슴
83 / 좋아하는 과일
85 / 고구마
87 / 딸아이 생일
89 / 외줄낚시
91 / 둥지
93 / 부부
95 / 진심
97 / 염원
99 / 주인공
101 / 추억은 파도처럼
103 / 님과 함께
105 / 하루살이의 기도

Part 3   Even in the Broken Pieces of a Jar

108 / Humans on Earth
112 / You and I
116 / Wings
118 / The Swan Woman
120 / Even in the Broken Pieces of a Jar
122 / The Children of the Monastery
124 / A Tree with Deep Roots
126 / First Kiss
128 / Stress Doesn't Exist
130 / The Scent of Chestnut Flowers
132 / Waiting for Spring
134 / As the Year Comes to a Close
136 / Mystical Honey
138 / Sending Off the Royal Chef
142 / The Great Doctor
144 / Cellphone
146 / The Thinking Reed
148 / On a Blank Sheet of Paper
150 / Universal Values
152 / Pioneering
156 / Consolation
158 / Poetry
160 / Poetry Creation
162 / Song of Duino

제3부   깨진 항아리 조각에도

109 / 지구상의 인간들
113 / 너와 나
117 / 날개
119 / 백조의 여인
121 / 깨진 항아리 조각에도
123 / 수도원의 아이들
125 / 뿌리 내린 나무
127 / 첫 키스
129 / 스트레스는 없다
131 / 밤꽃 향기
133 / 봄을 기다리며
135 / 한 해를 보내며
137 / 신비한 꿀
139 / 요리 상궁을 보내며
143 / 명의
145 / 휴대폰
147 / 생각하는 갈대
149 / 하얀 백지 위에
151 / 보편적 가치
153 / 개척
157 / 위로
159 / 시詩
161 / 시작詩作
163 / 두이노의 노래

Part 1
A Joyful Journey Together

제 1 부
함께하는 기쁜 여행

Three Prayers

Breathlessness on the highway,
standing suddenly at the threshold of life and death
I, with a desperate heart,
can only offer earnest prayers.
The hospital, just ten minutes away-
felt unbearably distant.

I felt guilty for my wife who arrived in a far and unfamiliar place,

Two tumors in my liver,
a thunderbolt of news,
tension creeping in like an unshakable fear,
a wandering of regrets that keeps my eyes shut.

My body, unable to withstand
the passing of time.
Without a moment to say "I love you,"
my hands trembled alone.
A desperate prayer swirling in an empty heart.

세 번의 기도

고속도로에서 일으킨 호흡곤란
갑작스런 생사의 문 앞에 선
나
애타는 마음에
간절한 기도뿐
10분 거리의 병원이 너무 멀었다

멀고도 먼 곳
낯선 길 찾아온
아내에게 미안한 마음이 앞섰다

간 속에 종양 두 개
날벼락 같은 소리에 무섭게 다가오는 긴장
눈을 뜰 수 없는 회한의 방황

흐르는 세월을 이겨내지 못한
나의 육신
사랑한다는 한마디 말 전할 겨를 없이
두 손만 떨릴 뿐
간절한 기도가 공전하는 공허한 마음

Both joy and hope were gone,
and only fear remained to hold on to

Through tears flowing like a waterfall,
memories flashed like a passing lantern.
In my desperate heart,
wishing for just five more years,
two prayers rise and overwhelm me.

Finally,
a lifeline was thrown to rescue me from the swamp of anxiety.

Having been immersed in a peaceful life,
volunteering and hobbies
stitched meaning into my passing years.

Now for myself,
I make three prayers
that will never truly end—

Saying the world has not yet ended.

기쁨도 희망도 잘려 나가고
두려운 마음만 붙들고 있을 때

폭포수같이 흐르는 눈물 속을
주마등처럼 스치는 추억
5년 만이라도 더 살 수 있도록
은총을 원하는 간절한 마음에
두 번의 기도가 나를 덮쳤다

드디어
불안의 늪에서 구출될 생명줄이 던져졌다

평화로운 삶에 물들게 되어
봉사와 취미 생활이
지나온 세월의 역사 歷史를
꾸미게 되었다

이제 나를 위해
떼를 쓰며
끝낼 수 없는 세 번의 기도를 한다

세상이 아직 끝나지 않았다고

A Joyful Journey Together

When the season of blooming flowers arrives,
Let's embark on a journey together.

Amid the pretty butterflies that come to find you,
and the whispers of their secret language,
Our hearts will be filled with joy.

In the season when red grapes ripen,
Let us love together.

With the scent of sweet wine,
redder than the glow of sunset,
I will set your heart ablaze.

No matter how often we look back,
There will be no journey as joyful as this.
Let's embark on the journey of life together.

함께하는 기쁜 여행

꽃 피는 계절이 오면
함께 여행을 떠나요

그대 찾아드는 예쁜 나비들과
속삭이는 언어 속에
기쁨이 가득하겠지요

붉은 포도가 익어가는 계절에서
우리 함께 사랑을 해요

노을빛보다 더 붉은
달콤한 포도주 향기로
당신의 가슴이 타오르게 할 것입니다

아무리 되돌아봐도
이처럼 즐거운 여행이 없게
함께 인생의 여행을 떠나요

Still, I Must Go

Snow is falling.
I can hardly see ahead.
When the snow falls too heavily,
The climb cannot begin.

Many make their way down,
their journey seeming meaningless.

I pause on my path upward,
turning back, lost in thought.

My footprints are covered in white,
And somehow,
The road I traveled feels sorrowful.

Knowing danger lurks ahead,
Still, I walk toward the summit once more.

그래도 가야지

눈이 내립니다
앞이 잘 보이지 않습니다
심하게 눈이 내리면
산행이 시작되지 않습니다

하산을 하는 사람이 많이 보입니다
산행에는 큰 의미가 없습니다

오르던 길을 잠시 멈추고
되돌아 보며 고민에 빠집니다

지나온 발자국들이 하얗게 채워지고
어쩜
왔던 길이 서럽게 느껴집니다

위험이 도사리고 있는 것을 알면서
나는 정상을 향해 다시 걸어가고 있습니다

The Heart That Sends Off

It feels like the final lesson at a beloved place of learning.
Like a dry leaf clinging to a late autumn tree,
a bittersweet feeling seeps in.

Even the sound of doves crying in the cold wind
carries the weight of sorrow.

Through rain or snow,
we always laughed together—
teachers and friends.
Though our time was brief,
I will cherish it dearly.

Like the boys of Alsace-Lorraine,
I swallow the surge of emotions
and manage to speak my final farewell.

Just as spring returns,
may the light of our love for poetry never fade.
May our precious verses
continue to flow eternally
to the farthest reaches of the universe.

떠나보내는 마음

정든 배움터의 마지막 수업 같아
늦가을 가로수에 매달린 마른 잎처럼
짠한 마음이 스며듭니다

찬바람에 울어대는 비둘기 소리조차
슬픔으로 들립니다

비가 오나 눈이 오나
항상 웃으면서 함께한
선생님과 친구들
짧은 인연이지만 소중히 간직하렵니다

알자스 로렌의 소년들처럼
솟구쳐 오르는 감정을 겨우 삼키며
마지막 인사말을 꺼냅니다

봄이 다시 오듯이
시$_{詩}$를 사랑하는 마음의 등불 꺼지지 않게
우리의 고귀한 시$_{詩}$들이
우주의 어느 끝자락에서도
고이고이 이어지기를 원합니다

A Long Journey

At the third dock,
my mother stood,
waving endlessly
as she bid me farewell.

When the sound of the ship's horn
echoes again tomorrow,
I will set off on another long journey.

Like my mother's waving hands,
I, too, wave toward my family,
as if to say,

Stay well and be healthy.

긴 여행

제3선착장에서
두 손 하염없이 흔들며
배웅해 주셨던 어머니
생각이 떠오른다

뱃고동 소리가
내일 들려오면
나는 또다시 긴 여행을 떠날 것이다

어머니가 흔들던 손 닮아
나도 가족을 향해
손을 흔든다

몸 건강히 잘 있어 달라고

Prayer and Answer

On my journey through Europe,
I offer a prayer to the Virgin Mary.

My wife asks
what I am praying for,
so earnestly and for so long.

I tell her
that I pray for our journey together
to be a blessed path in life.

Prayers may take many forms,
but for the peace of the road ahead,
the answer is already given.

기도와 대답

유럽 여행길에서
성모 마리아에게 기도 한다

무슨 기도를 그토록 진지하게
오래 하는지
동행한 아내가 묻는다

당신과 함께하는 여행이
복된 삶의 여정이 되라고
기도 드린다고 말했다

기도는 다양할 수 있으나
남은 여정의 평화를 위해
대답은 이미 정해져 있었다

Oceania Journey

My soul,
drawn by an intense emerald glow,
sets off on this journey.

In the Waitomo Caves,
where I first arrived,
countless fireflies gleamed brightly,
guiding the lost travelers as if they were
stars in the night sky.

At the beautiful Opera House,
a white boat carried dreams on its deck,
made from stacked seashells.
It played Dvořák's magnificent symphony
with the harmony of waves,
rushing toward the Milky Way.

Yesterday,
heavy rain fell over Sydney.

오세니아 여정

내 영혼이
강렬한 에메랄드빛에
이끌리듯 떠난 여행

처음 만난
와이토모 동굴에는
수없이 많은 반딧불이가
길을 잃은 나그네를 안내하듯
아름다운 별빛처럼 반짝이고 있었습니다

하얀 조각배에 꿈을 실은
조개껍데기를 쌓아 만든
예쁜 오페라하우스에서는
은하수를 향해 달리는
파도의 하모니가
드보르작의 멋진 교향곡을
연주하고 있었습니다

어제는
시드니에 많은 비가 내렸습니다

Today,
a beautiful rainbow rises
above the Three Sisters peaks of the Blue Mountains.
It feels like life rides its own rhythm.

For tomorrow's splendid twilight journey,
I am now crossing the Harbour Bridge.

오늘은
블루마운틴 세 자매 봉우리 위로
아름다운 무지개가
솟아오릅니다
고유한 리듬을 타는 인생같습니다

나는 내일로 예정된
멋진 황혼의 여정을 위해
지금 하버브릿지를 건너고 있습니다

A Life Like an Arrow

To search for gold,
I set out for a distant land
where white clouds linger.

In the autumn fields of Queenstown,
when ripe grains fill the barns,
I send joyful news via a dove,
hurrying to my family.

My parents have long passed,
and my beloved,
weary from waiting,
left for distant lands a long time ago.

Returned home,
an old man with white hair, muttering to himself
as he stares into the mirror.

Time, like an arrow,
has flown by quickly.

화살 같은 인생

황금을 찾으러
흰 구름이 머무는 먼 땅으로
길을 떠났다

퀸스타운Queens town 가을 벌판에는 잘 익은 곡식들이
곳간을 가득 채우고 있을 때
비둘기에 기쁜 소식을 실어
가족에게 급히 날려 보낸다

부모님은 벌써 돌아가셨고
사랑하는 이도
기다림에 지쳐 먼 곳으로
떠난 지 한참 후가 되었다

집으로 돌아와
웬 백발노인이 혼자 중얼거리며
거울을 쳐다보고 있다

세월은
쏜살같이 빨랐다

At the Terminus

Have you seen
the conversation between reality and shadow?

It is not a dialogue dividing the past from the present,
but the awkward conversation between
those who are leaving and those who will stay —it is
mysterious.

In an ordinary tone,
they were worrying about tomorrow,
which will quickly vanish.

Because it is intertwined with unknown labyrinths
there was encouragement within.
So, standing at the terminus,
I tightly grasp the shadow's hand.

종점에서

실체와 그림자가
서로 이야기 하는 것을 보았습니까?

과거와 현재를 나누는 대화도 아니고
떠나는 자와 남아 있는 자의
어색한 말투가 신비롭습니다

일상적인 말투로
홀연히 사라지고 마는 내일을
걱정하며 말을 나눕니다

알지 못할 미로도 섞여 있기에
그 속에는 격려가 있고
나는 종점에 서서
그림자의 손을 꼭 잡아주었습니다

The Empty Journey

Like a squirrel running on its wheel,
in the life I live,
I set off on a journey,
searching for a path with new meaning.

Beyond the Alps,
even when I visit the monastery,
the saints found in the candlelight have no words.

In the gods' garden
that rules the Pacific,
only the hot sun and dry grains
of sand remain.

When I feel a gust of wind
born from the inertia of the universe,
the autumn journey passes by,
quietly and without sound.

허무한 여정

다람쥐 쳇바퀴 돌듯
살아가는 삶 속에서
새로운 의미가 있는 길 찾아
여행을 떠난다

알프스산 넘어
수도원을 둘러봐도
촛불 속에서 찾은 성인들은 말이 없다

태평양을 지배하고 있는
신들의 정원에는
뜨거운 태양과 무미건조한
모래알뿐

우주의 관성에서 생겨나는
한 줄기 바람을 느낄 때
가을 여정이
소리 없이 지나가고 있었다

Tears-soaked Bread

On the plane,
no matter how far I go,
it feels like an endless journey
through a foreign land.

In the heart of a goose flying,
there is full of only loneliness.

Sitting alone on a cold bench
in a foreign land
with fallen leaves swirling around,

I put a piece of bread in my mouth,
but the yearning grows stronger.

Like hot tears falling
from the leaves,
The river flows with the determination for success

눈물 젖은 빵

비행기에 올라
가도 가도 끝없는
이국의 고행길

기러기 되어 날아가는 심정에
외로움만 가득하다

이국땅에서
가랑잎 흩날리는 늦가을
싸늘한 벤치에 홀로 앉아
빵 조각 하나 입에 넣어봐도
울컥 고파지는 그리움

나뭇잎처럼 뚝뚝 떨어지는
뜨거운 눈물
성공의 결심에 흐르는 강물

The Spirit of the Indian

Riding the fresh breeze washed by spring rain,
I go to meet my brothers with yellow faces.

Living happily in the embrace of
the sky, earth, and trees,
people who love nature
praying toward the sun.

Wounded by the tide of
immense civilization,
they become yellow caterpillars,
trapped in cocoons,
lonely brothers.

Were they not the brothers who, since ancient times,
believed the footsteps of reindeer were the truth?

Just as winter passes and spring arrives,
the spirits of those who honor the natural order
never disappear.
Instead, they rise again,
in the form of a beautiful yellow butterfly,
soaring back into the sky.

인디언 정령精靈

봄비에 씻겨진 상큼한 바람 타고
노란 얼굴을 가진 형제를 만나러 간다

하늘과 땅과 나무들의 품속에서
행복하게 살아오며
태양을 향해 기도하는
자연을 사랑하는 사람들

밀물처럼 밀려드는
거대한 문명 속에 상처받고
노란 애벌레 되어
고치 속에 갇혀버린
외로운 형제들

예부터 순록의 발자국을 진리라 믿고
살아온 형제들이 아니었던가

겨울이 가고 봄이 오듯
순리를 존중하는 거룩한 존재들의 정령은
결코 사라지지 않고
아름다운 노란 나비의 영혼으로
다시 하늘로 날아 오른다

To That Place

Throwing open the wooden gate,
I step into a place where my parents welcome me,
where my beloved relatives await.

A lullaby drifts in,
a song of the soul,
bringing waves of happiness, like the rising tide.

When the tasks given to me
are finally complete,
I wish to return, like one going home,
to that eternal place I long for.

With the sound of sacred prayers,
I will rest for a moment
on the Milky Way, flowing beneath the starlight,
before departing for that everlasting place.

그곳으로

사립문을 활짝 열고
나를 반겨주실 부모님과
보고 싶은 친지들이 계시는 곳

자장가를 불러주는
영혼의 노래가
파도처럼 밀려오는 행복감을 가져다 줍니다

주어진
모든 일들이 끝나는 날
고향 가듯 그립고 영원한 집으로
돌아가고 싶습니다

거룩한 기도 소리
별빛 따라 흐르는 은하수에
잠시 머물다 영원한 그곳으로 떠나렵니다

Autumn Reflections

It feels like just yesterday that spring arrived,
yet the chapel bells now chime, heralding autumn—
how lonely it sounds.

On each branch, abundant fruits
pray beneath the autumn sunlight,
clinging tightly, striving to grow sweeter.

The shortened days summon dusk,
and those who have finished their harvest early
follow the starlight,
making their way home.

With thoughts of my mother's warm embrace,
I walk through the changing season.

가을 사념思念

봄을 맞이한 지가 어제 같은데
가을을 알리는 예배당 종소리
참으로 쓸쓸합니다

가지마다 탐스러운 과일들은
가을 햇살에 기도하며
단맛을 더하기 위해
매달려 있습니다

짧아진 해가 땅거미를 부르고
일찍 추수를 마친 사람들은
별빛을 따라
집으로 돌아갑니다

다정하게 반겨주실 어머니를 생각하며
걸어가는 계절이 되었습니다

The Swing

With a gentle step,
I hop on and push forward—
suddenly, the whole world unfolds before me.

As my feet soar
toward the sky,
billowing clouds slip beneath my dress.

In the rhythm of repetitive motion,
beads of sweat dance and fall,
yet laughter never leaves my lips.

Is this celestial journey,
one I've never seen before,
already coming to an end?
My hands and feet grow weary,
and love rushes past, fleeting as ever.

그네

살짝
올라타서 힘차게 구르면
먼 세상까지 다 보인다

두 발바닥이
하늘을 향해 솟구치면
뭉게구름이 치마 속으로 들어온다

반복되는 리듬 속에서
뜨거운 땀들이 춤을 추며
끝없이 흘러내려도
환호성이 입가를 떠나지 않는다

여태껏 보지 못한 별천지 여행도
벌써 끝이 나는 건지
손과 발에 힘이 사그라들고
사랑은 빠르게 지나가고 있다

Silver Elegy

When frost descends,
the weight of years drifts
further from the world.

On late autumn strolls,
two paths always appear before me.

Like the Voyager,
yearning to escape this realm,
I set forth on a road
laden with philosophy and faith—
yet the journey is far from over.

Or I may stand like the ancient pine of Tongdo Temple,
anchored by the gravity of life,
held firm by the inertia of time.

But if both roads converge
at the end of a single path,
then does the choice truly matter?
Silvered hair sways in quiet confusion.

은빛 엘리지

서리가 내리면
연륜은 세상으로부터
점점 멀어져 간다

늦가을 산책길에 오르면
언제나 두 갈래 길이 나타난다

보이저호처럼
속세를 탈출 하고자
철학과 신앙을 실은 길
아직 멀다

통도사 노송처럼
지루한 관성으로 삶의 중력을
굳건히 지탱하는 길도 있지만

두 길이 어차피 한 길에서
만난다고 생각하면
어느 길이 중요한지
은빛의 머리가 혼란해 진다

Serenade of November

With the deep call of a horn,
the ship's wake vanishes
without a trace
upon the blue sea.

Outside the window,
the sound of late autumn raindrops
becomes the song that I sing for you
before December arrives.

Even the splendid garments of the season
scatter with the passing wind,
and the migrating birds
have all departed.

Yet, our journey through life together,
wings flapping in brilliance,
sails toward the evening glow.

Before November fades,
from your window,
my serenade echoes ceaselessly.

11월의 세레나데

큰 뱃고동 소리를 내며
지나온 항적들이
푸른 바닷물 위에서
흔적 없이 사라진다

창밖에 떨어지는
늦가을 낙수 소리
12월이 오기 전에
당신을 향해 부르는 나의 노래

화려한 계절의 옷조차
지나가는 바람에 흩날리며
철새들도 모두 떠나고 있다

당신과 함께하는 삶의 여정
화려하게 날갯짓하며
저녁노을 향해 가고 있지 않는가

당신의 창가에서
11월이 가기 전
끊임없이 소야곡을 부르고 있다

Footprints on the Snow

Snow falls—
on my head,
on my heart,
covering all in white.

Within my heart, traces remain, never fading.
Above my head, memories linger, never forgotten.
Snow blankets everything in pure white.

When the warmth of love and hope rises again,
the white snow
covers the earth.

With every footprint disappearing beneath the snow,
the season deepens into crimson hues,
as the flowers of twilight bloom in beauty.

눈 위의 발자국

눈이 내린다
머리에도
마음에도
하얗게 내린다

마음속에는 사라지지 않는 흔적
머리 위에는 잊히지 않는 추억
눈이 하얗게 내려 덮이고 있다

뜨거운 사랑의 소망이 다시 피어오르면
하얀 눈이
대지를 덮는다

하얗게 덮여 가는 발자국마다
붉게 물들어 가는 계절
아름다운 황혼의 꽃들이 피어나고 있다

The Disappearance of a Model

With heavy makeup and long lashes,
she walks, gazing at the rainbow.
Her clothes are a symbol of freedom.

A woman wears a hijab.
Behind the temple and cathedral,
a kindergarten comes into view.
The lens's field of vision has widened.

In the clicking sound of shutters,
a life had been tamed
like a monkey—
only wings have begun to sprout.

To a place without phones,
without credit cards,
without computers,
I long to soar high,
following the pink-hued sunset.

모델의 실종

짙은 화장에 커다란 속눈썹
무지개를 응시하며 걷는다
옷은 자유의 상징이다

여인이 쓴 히잡
절과 성당 뒤에는 유치원이 보인다
렌즈의 시야가 넓어졌다

찰깍거리는 소리 속에
원숭이처럼 길들여
달려온 삶
돋아나는 것은 날개뿐

휴대폰도, 신용카드도
컴퓨터도 없는 곳으로
분홍빛 노을 따라
높이 높이 날아오르고 싶다

Eyelids

At the entrance of Tongdo Temple,
an old pine tree, its spine bent by time,
draws a weary curve.

Before Naewon Temple,
an aged zelkova leans on its cane,
its legs bowed by the years.

Here and there,
creaking voices cry out,
yet even a patch brings no relief.

Is anything in this world
heavier than one's own eyelids?

The weight of time,
the pain of life—
as if to soothe them all,
my eyes slowly drift shut.

눈꺼풀

세월에 등뼈가 휘어진
통도사 입구의 노송
피곤한 곡선을 그린다

세월에 다리가 휘어진
내원사 앞 느티나무도
지팡이를 짚고 있다

이곳저곳
삐거덕대는 아우성
파스를 붙여도 소용이 없다

세상에서
제일 무거운 것이
눈꺼풀이 아닌가

세월의 무게도
삶의 아픔도
잠재우듯 눈이 스르르 감겨져 내린다

Feast

The hearts of train passengers,
each carrying different emotions,
are watched by the cosmos flowers
blooming along the tracks.

On the path of seeking the meaning of love,
with a pure heart,
there stood trials
and crosses to bear—
it was never an easy journey.

Venus became the symbol of beauty,
yet disorder lingers within,
and even the radiant rainbow in the sky
has a fleeting nature.

Not every woman
veiled in delicate lace is truly beautiful—
a single red rose shines brighter.
For within unmasked nature,
true beauty crystallizes.

향연

서로 틀린 감정을 가진
기차 승객의 마음
선로 따라 피어있는 코스모스가 보고있다

순결한 마음으로
사랑의 의미를 찾아 헤매던 길
앞에는 고행도
십자가도 서 있어
언제나 쉬운 일 아니었다

비너스는 아름다움의 대명사가 되었지만
무질서가 내재해 있고
하늘의 영롱한 무지개조차
쉽게 사라지는 습성을 가지고 있다

예쁜 망사를 쓰고 있는 여인이 모두
아름다운 것이 아니고
붉은 장미꽃 한 송이가 더 눈부시다
숨김없는 자연 속에는
아름다운 결정체가 있기 때문이다

Physical love driven by desire
may be trapped in the unseen net
forged by Hephaestus,
or pierced by the spears of jealousy.

A night without a passionate hug
brings a trembling fear
like drifting, lost in the universe,

Even when I reach out with open arms,
I grasp only empty space.
A place without meetings or farewells,
where even the self is lost—
A world without true love,
a world of indifference, is sorrowful.

욕망으로 이루어진 육체적 사랑은
헤파이스토스가 만든
눈에 보이지 않는 그물에 갇히기도 하고
질투의 창들이 날아들기도 한다

뜨거운 포옹이 없는 밤은
항상 우주에 미아가 된 듯
무서움에 떤다

두 팔을 벌려 잡으려 해도
잡히지 않는 공허한 공간
만남이나 헤어짐이 없는 곳
자아조차 잃어버리는
진정한 사랑이 없는
무심의 세계가 슬프다

Part 2
The Nest

제 2 부
둥 지

A Quiet Countryside Sketch

Seated at a hilltop café, I gaze out
at the picture-perfect terraced rice fields.

Like freshly combed hair,
the rice stalks stand neatly in rows,
and wherever white birds roam,
it feels like home.

For those who see farming as their calling,
who have spent a lifetime in the fields,
their wrinkled faces are etched along
the winding paths of the rice paddies.

Carrying a tray of delicious refreshments,
a mother walks toward me—
her warm longing
comes to me, who can never forget.

고즈넉한 시골의 소묘

언덕 위 카페에 앉아 바라보면
그림같이 예쁜 계단식 논들

금방 빗질한 듯
벼들이 정갈하게 심겨져있고
하얀 새가 노니는 곳은
어디든지 고향을 느끼게 한다

농사를 천직으로 생각하고
평생을 논에서 살다가
굽어진 논두렁길 따라 새겨진
주름진 얼굴

맛있는 새참을 이고
걸어오는 어머니의 따뜻한 그리움이
잊지 못하는 나에게로 오고 있다

My Wife's Footprints

Snow falls,
covering even all the joys and sorrows
of the world in white.

When I turn back with longing,
all I see are the traces of the footsteps.

Beside my large footprints,
the weary yet steadfast ones that followed—
they were yours.

아내의 발자국

눈이 내립니다
세상의 모든 기쁨과 슬픔조차
하얗게 덮혀집니다

아쉬워 뒤돌아보면
걸어온 두 발자국 흔적만 보입니다

큰 발자국 옆에서 힘들게 따라온
고마운 발자국
당신이었습니다

Together

For the first time in a while,
I came to the library with my youngest.

Not even an hour had passed,
I received the signal—
it was time to leave.

Closing our books,
we step outside,
off to find something delicious to eat.

In life,
which matters more—
what is interesting or what is delicious?

함께

모처럼 막내와 도서관에 왔습니다

한 시간도 안 되었는데
밖으로 나가자는
신호가 왔습니다

책을 덮고
맛있는 것 사 먹으러
도서관을 나섭니다

우리의 삶에 있어서
재미있는 것과 맛있는 것 중
어느 것이 더 중요한지요!

Badminton Story

On a day when the morning sunlight
brightly illuminates the calendar,
I enjoy a badminton match with
my youngest, Yoonjin, who is dressed in yellow.

With the shuttlecock, its wings soaring,
we send each other's wishes flying high,
laughing endlessly together,
my daughter and I—an amazing team.

In the ongoing rally,
I realize how quickly the day is passing.
Over the rising net,
her face, as beautiful as the full moon,
appears, my lovely daughter, Yoonjin.

Even when white clouds rush in
and the faint starlight is hidden,
when the dark night falls,
our badminton game will continue,
forever bright, within the treasured memories.

배드민턴 이야기

아침 햇살이 카렌다를
밝게 비추는 날
노란색 옷을 입은 막내 윤진이와
배드민턴 경기를 즐긴다

날개가 달린 셔틀콕에
서로의 염원을 싣고
하늘 높이 힘차게 날려 보내며
웃음이 끊이지 않는 딸아이와 나
환상의 콤비다

이어지는 렐리 속에 하루가 얼마나
빠르게 흘러가는지
높아져 가는 네트 위로
보름달처럼
예쁜 딸아이 윤진이의 얼굴이 떠오른다

하얀 구름이 밀려와
희미한 별빛마저 가리우는
캄캄한 밤이 와도
영원히 밝을 추억 속에서
배드민턴 놀이는
계속 이어질 것이다

When May Comes

Letting go of my mother's hand,
I journey forward alone,
once again welcoming May.

Through countless nights of stumbling,
her smile, warm as the full moon,
has always been
a guiding light.

In this season of lush greenery,
petals fall first,
and with the wind,
my beloved mother drifts away.

Each time I cried aloud,
she always came running.
Now, I long to bury my face
in May's embrace
and weep to my heart's content.

5월이 오면

어머니의 손을 놓고
홀로 달려가는 여정
또다시 5월을 맞이합니다

수없이 비틀거렸던 밤길
보름달처럼 푸근한
어머니의 미소가 언제나
환한 등불이 되었습니다

실록이 우거져 오는 계절에는
꽃잎이 먼저 떨어지고
바람 따라
훌쩍 떠나버린 그리운 어머니

큰소리 내어 울 때마다
언제나 달려오셨던 기억
오월의 품속에 얼굴을 파묻고
실컷 울고 싶습니다

Chuseok Sketch

In the season when grains and fruits ripen in abundance,
under the radiant full moon,
its halo glows ever so beautifully.

Before the bountiful ancestral table,
I bow deeply with heartfelt gratitude
to my revered ancestors,
whose love remains unchanged.

Gathered warmly together,
we share drinks over delicious food,
exchanging stories of harmony,
as the rich aroma of tradition lingers in the air.

Before we know it, autumn has seeped into our souls.
As we welcome Chuseok once again,
bathed in the golden light of the harvest,
we pray that life may ripen beautifully.
And when the bright, full moon rises high,
we bring our hands together in quiet reverence.

추석 소묘

오곡백과가 탐스럽게 익는 계절
휘영청 밝은 달밤
달무리가 유난히 곱다

푸짐한 차례상 앞에
변함없이 사랑해 주시는
존경하는 조상님
정성을 다해
감사의 큰절을 올린다

정겹게 둘러앉아
맛있는 음식들 사이로
술 한 잔씩 권하며 나누는
화목한 이야기
맛깔스레 피어오르는 향기

어느덧 가을 깊숙이 스며든 우리의 영혼
가을이 되면 맞이하는 한가위에
풍요로운 햇살 속에서
삶이 곱게 영글어 가도록
밝고 커다란 보름달이 떠오르면
두 손을 조용히 모은다

Scent of My Father

Somewhere,
a familiar scent
beckons my steps.

Though the air is not yet cold,
I quietly draw near
to someone warming themselves by the fire,
seeking its gentle heat.

Memories rise like white smoke,
drifting beyond the western hills,
while a tide of loneliness
swells deep as the abyss.

Before I know it,
my father's familiar scent
has settled into me—
an everlasting longing.

아버지의 향내

어디선가
낯익은 냄새에
발길이 따라 나선다

아직 쌀쌀한 날씨는 아니지만
불을 쬐고 있는 사람 곁으로
살그머니 다가가 온기를 느껴 본다

추억은 하얀 연기 되어
서산으로 넘어가고
밀려오는 외로움은
심연처럼 깊다

어느새 내 몸에 스며든
아버지의 익숙한 체취
영원한 그리움으로 남아있다

To My Son

Breaking free from the shell,
you marvel at the vast sky,
the breathtaking heights,
and the endless forests filled with wonder.

Nestled in your mother's embrace,
you have grown,
busy nurturing the days
with purpose and meaning.

Within your heart,
the wings of your soul take shape—
may they grow with wisdom and courage.

And when the steadfast winds rise,
soar boldly into the sky,
spread your great wings like an eagle,
gazing upon the world with hope,
rising ever higher.

아들에게

알을 깨고 나온 세상
하늘이 얼마나 높은지 놀라운 광경
세상에 널려있는 아름다운 숲들
모든 것이 경이롭다

둥지 튼 엄마 품속에서
자라온 너
보람된 날들을 가꾸기에 바쁘다

네 가슴 속에서
자라나는 영혼의 날개
지혜와 용맹으로 자라나거라

굳건한 바람이 불어오는 날이면
힘차게 창공에 올라
독수리처럼 큰 날개를 펴
희망으로 세상을 바라보며
높이 더 높이 날기 바란다

Aching Heart

A scolded child
sobs even in sleep.

Drifting off without easing the sorrow
feels unbearably heartbreaking.

I was a child full of sadness,
whimpering even in the morning
my mother left.

Unable to embrace all that sorrow,
you had to embark on a distant journey.
You must have hurt even more than I did—
just the thought of it
makes my heart ache.

아픈 가슴

야단맞은 아이가 잠 속에서까지
훌쩍거립니다

억울함을 풀지 못한 채
잠이 든 것이
무척 안쓰럽게 느꼈습니다

서러움이 유난히 많던 나
어머니가 떠나버린 아침까지
훌쩍였습니다

그 맘 다 품어주지 못한 채
먼 길을 떠나야 할 당신
나보다 더욱 아팠겠지요
생각만 해도 가슴이 저며 옵니다

My Favorite Fruit
- A Letter from Lee Yoon-jin to Dad -

Dad asks me what my favorite fruit is.

Between bananas, oranges, and apples,
which one should I choose?
For a moment, I feel puzzled.

I like them all,
but how should I rank them?
My heart hesitates.

Bananas have a lovely fragrance,
oranges have a beautiful color,
and apples make a delightful crunch when eaten—
I can't leave out a single one.

Perhaps understanding my thoughts,
Dad gently pats my head.

좋아하는 과일
- 아빠에게 보내는 이윤진의 글 -

어떤 과일이 좋은지 물으시는 아빠

바나나, 오렌지, 사과 중
어느 과일이 좋을지
어리둥절한 순간

나는 다 좋아하는데
순서를 어떻게 해야 하나
망설이는 마음

향기가 좋은 바나나
색깔이 좋은 오렌지
사각사각 먹을 때
소리가 좋게 나는 사과라서
하나도 빼놓을 수 없는 과일들

내 마음을 아는지 아빠는 제 머리를
쓰다듬어 주셨다

Sweet Potatoes

With every tug on the vine,
large and small clusters emerge.
Are they stems? Or roots?

Returning from school,
I am warmly greeted
by fragments of childhood memories.

As the bamboo gate swings open,
a sweet aroma drifts in,
and the first bite of a roasted sweet potato
feels so familiar, so dear.

Even as frost settles on my hair,
each one unearthed
brings forth a deep purple longing,
etched in memory,
carrying the happiness of my youth.

고구마

당기는 줄기마다 딸려 나오는
크고 작은 덩어리
줄기인가요? 뿌리인가요?

학교에서 돌아오면
반가이 맞이해주는 고향
추억의 편린들

사릿대 문이 열리고
달콤한 향내가 스며들면
한입 베어 문 고구마가 정겹다

머리에 흰서리가 내려도
하나씩 딸려 나오는
자주색 그리움
또렷이 추억으로 남아 있어
유년의 행복을 이어준다

Daughter's Birthday

Filled with the greenness of April,
what I've been eagerly waiting for,
could it be because of the delicious cake?

On April 23rd, the day my daughter was beautifully born,
the single parent families gathers together,
lighting candles, clapping,
and filling the space with a gentle song.

Even when the wind blows and
rainy days come,
always hold hope in your heart,
and remember that the path you walk is a flower road.
I bless you with a smile.

딸아이 생일

4월의 푸르름을 듬뿍 담아
손꼽아 기다리는 것은
맛있는 케익 때문일까?

딸애가 예쁘게 태어난 4월 23일
기러기 가족들이 한곳에 모여
촛불을 켜고 박수치며
다정스러운 노래로 공간을 채운다

바람이 불고
비 오는 날이 되어도
항상 마음만은 희망을 간직하며
걷는 길이 꽃길이라 생각하고 걸어가라고
웃음으로 축복해 본다

Single-Line Fishing

When my mind becomes complicated, sometimes,
I go to the reservoir
and fish.

The familiar people
place several fishing rods
and wait for the fish.

I, waiting on a single line,
pour all my attention into the fishing.

Rather than living entangled
in complexity,
it is more joyful to live simply.

I cast my love on the single line,
and with a focused gaze,
I look at one place,
my heart, red and pure.

외줄낚시

마음이 복잡해질 때
가끔
저수지에 가서
낚시를 한다

익숙한 사람들은
여러 개의 낚싯대를 놓고
물고기를 기다린다

하나의 낚싯대에 매달려 기다리는
나
외줄낚시에 온 정성을 기울인다

복잡하게
얽히고 설키면서
살아가는 것보다
단순하게 살아가는 것이 즐겁다

외줄낚시에 사랑을 드리우고
오롯이 한 곳을 바라보는
붉은 내 마음

Nest

With a heart full of excitement, I gently hold your hand,
and unknowingly, I see the calluses formed over time,
the traces of the years embedded within.

In the secret garden we walk through,
yellow lilacs bloom beautifully.

When we turn our steps back
toward the rear garden,
five crimson roses
bloom gracefully.

On the distant ridges of the mountains,
cherry blossoms and nightingales sing,
and with joy in my heart,
I walk and walk, towards the season ahead.

둥지

설레는 마음으로 살며시 잡은 손
나도 몰래 굳은살 알알이 박여있는
세월의 흔적을 들여다본다

함께 거니는 비원祕苑에는
노란 라일락이
예쁘게 피어나고 있다

다정히 걸어가는 발걸음을
후원後苑으로 돌렸을 때
담홍빛 장미 5송이
우아하게 피어나고

멀리 보이는 산등성이에
산벚꽃도 소쩍새도 노래하는 계절을 향해
환희에 찬 걸음을 걷고 걷는다

Couple

When an easy or difficult time arises,
you rush to me like lightning,
quietly holding my hand,
offering comfort and encouragement.

Whether joy or sorrow comes,
you laugh and cry with me.

With a heart burning fiercely,
the flames of love
never cease.

부부

쉽거나 어려운 일 생기면
번개같이 달려와
조용히 내 손을 잡고
위로하며 격려해 준 사람

기쁘거나 슬픈일이 생겨도
함께 웃고 울어 준 사람

활활 타오르는 가슴
사랑의 불길이
멈출 새 없다

Sincerity

In the long shadow we walk together,
a feeling of apology lies scattered.

You, by my side,
become the autumn sunlight,
and the time spent preparing for winter is pure joy.

The gift I've hidden in the sundial,
for you,
I want to live with the fun of
opening it one by one.

I am missing
your smile again today.

진심

함께 걷는
긴 그림자 속에
미안한 마음이 널려있다

곁에 있는 당신
가을 햇살 되어
겨울을 준비하는 시간이 마냥 즐겁다

해시계 속에 숨겨둔
당신을 위한 나의 선물
하나둘 열어보는 재미로 살고 싶은
나의 마음

나는 오늘도 당신의 미소를
그리고 있다

Aspiration

In the chilly late autumn,
the sound of the old monk's wooden gong
resonates through the mountain temple,
flowing along the valley.

Amid those praying in the temple hall
for the well-being of their families,
I
pray for myself.

A heartfelt prayer in the season of falling leaves—
wishing that happiness may forever flow
in the embrace of my loved ones.

염원

쌀쌀한 늦가을
노승의 목탁 소리가
흐르는 계곡 따라
산사에 울려 퍼진다

법당에서
가족을 위해 기도를 하는 사람 사이
나는
나를 위해 기도한다

낙엽 지는 계절의 간절한 기도
사랑하는 사람들의 품속에서
행복한 일들이 영원히 흐를 것을 바라고 있다

Protagonist

In the cold city,
it is difficult for beautiful women
to find their match.

I am a poet.

With warm words, I build a nest,
a garden for you,
where light endlessly shines.

You have become
the protagonist of the poem I write,
and that makes me happy.

주인공

차가운 도심에서
아름다운 여인들은
상대를 찾기가 매우 어렵습니다

나는 시인詩人

따스한 글로써 둥지를 만들고
계속 빛이 뿜어져 나오는
당신을 위한
정원을 만들고 있습니다

내가 쓰고 있는 시詩 속에
주인공이 된
당신
나는 행복합니다

Memories Like Waves

The mountains and fields, warm like a mother's embrace,
even keep the clouds lingering in the sky.

Though the people of the past
are no longer seen,
beloved ones return in waves of memory.

Drifting in as silent waves,
then fading away
like shimmering white crests.

추억은 파도처럼

엄마의 품속같이 포근한 산과 들이
구름조차 하늘에 머물게 합니다

옛 사람들이
더 이상 보이지 않아도
그리운 이들이 추억 속으로 밀려듭니다

소리 없는 파도 되어 밀려왔다가
가물가물 흰 물결로
되돌아갑니다

With You

If there is a burden to bear,
I will bear it with you.

In sorrow, we will hold each other tight,
crying together through the night.

In joy, we will embrace,
dancing without hesitation.

Under the night sky,
we will count the stars of love,
sharing this beautiful journey together.

님과 함께

힘 드는 일 있다면
함께 힘 들어 하겠습니다

슬플 땐 서로 부둥켜안고
밤새워 함께 울겠습니다

기쁜 일에는 얼싸안고
춤이라도 추겠습니다

밤하늘을 쳐다보고
사랑의 별을 세어가며
아름다운 여정旅情을 함께 나누고 있습니다

A Mayfly's Prayer

As the sunset paints the sky,
a fleeting body falls like white petals,
whispering the wisdom of nature's cycle.

With wings of creation's first flutter,
it cries out for salvation,
yet its final journey is to scatter—
leaving the meaning of life a mystery.

A mayfly, bearing both joy and sorrow,
is like my earnest prayer,
a devotion meant only for you.

The prayers that continue along this journey
are my desperate confession.

Mourning the severed time,
I fold my hands in sorrowful reverence.

하루살이의 기도

노을이 물들면
하얀 꽃잎처럼 떨어지는 육체에
자연 순리를 엿보게 합니다

태초 날갯짓으로
구원의 손길을 절규하지만
흩어져야 하는 마지막 여정
삶이 무엇인지 어리둥절케 합니다

환희와 질곡의 그림자를 가진 하루살이
당신만을 사랑하는
나의 간곡한 기도와 같습니다

여정旅程에서 이어지는 기도는
애절한 나의 고백

단절되는 시간이 애석哀惜해
두 손 모읍니다

Part 3
Even in the Broken Pieces of a Jar

제 3 부
깨진 항아리 조각에도

Humans on Earth

The Homo sapiens who escaped from Africa,
scattered across the corners of the Earth,
continue to produce gossip.

When boastful reporters spread rumors of the birth of God,
rocks and trees with various colors
form a rainbow-colored belt,
and tigers and bears eat garlic.

Into the red placard,
a flock of sheep enters,
and in the waters of Mesopotamia,
scarecrows, trapped like slaves,
pray fervently to God.

On a night when the crescent moon slowly disappears,
above the Kori Nuclear Power Plant,
countless stars twinkle like fireflies,
and the faces of the gods,
become the Messiah, announcing the birth of a new star.

지구상의 인간들

아프리카에서 탈출해 온 호모 사피엔스 무리들
지구 구석구석에 흩어져
뒷담화를 계속 생산한다

허풍쟁이 기자들이 신의 탄생을 소문낼 때
다양한 색깔을 가진 바위와 나무가
무지갯빛 띠를 두르면
호랑이와 곰은 마늘을 먹는다

붉은 플랜카드 안으로
양 떼가 들어가고
메소포타미아의 물줄기에
노예처럼 갇혀 버린 허수아비들
간절한 마음으로
신께 기도 올린다

초승 달빛이 서서히 사라지던 밤
고리 원자력 발전소 위에
수많은 별이 반딧불처럼 반짝이고
신들의 얼굴이
메시아가 되어 새로운 스타탄생을 알린다

Among all living creatures born with genes,
those born with horns,
while deer antlers are precious as medicine,
if they enter the sewer,
they spend the night telling terrifying monster stories.

유전자를 가지고 태어나는
모든 생명체 중
뿔을 가지고 태어난 피조물들
녹용은 귀한 약재로 쓰이지만
하수구로 들어가면
무서운 괴물 이야기로 밤을 새운다

You and I

The Renaissance caused the walls on both sides of the pyramid
to collapse.

The colors trapped inside
freed themselves onto the streets,
pouring out freely, wildly.

The fence of the beautiful cathedral is gone,
and the roses wander the streets,
seeking new jobs.

Following the shining star,
believing that I can find my mother,
the longing deepens.

At the tavern, they sell hamburgers,
and at the forge, they make Ferraris,
but can it become a new pyramid construction site?

너와 나

르네상스가 피라미드의 양쪽 벽을
무너지게 했다

그 속에 갇혀있던
다양한 색깔들이 해방된 길거리로
자유로이 마구 쏟아져 나왔다

아름답던 성당의 울타리가 없어지고
장미들은 새로운 일자리를 찾아
거리를 방황한다

빛나는 별을 따라가면
어머니를 찾을 수 있다는 믿음에
그리움이 더욱 짙다

주막에서 햄버거를 팔고
대장간에서 페라리를 만들어도
새로운 피라미드 건설 현장이 될 수 있을까

Bowing to fascism,
escaping from reality—
instead, beautiful stars of a new paradigm
begin to shine.

Into the terrifying world,
a fearful freedom that seems to throw me in!

But for the freedom I long for,
we
grasp the hand of truth and rising fresh!

파시즘에 고개 숙이고
현실을 도피하는 장면이 아닌
아름다운 신 패러다임의 별들이
반짝이기 시작한다

무서운 세상 속으로
나를 던져 버리는 듯한 두려운 자유!

그러나 갈망하는 자유를 위해
진실의 손을 맞잡고 풋풋하게 일어나는
사랑스런 너와 나!

Wings

A sharp wind that seems to scratch the back of my hand blows
at the edge of a cliff.
In a sunny spot, there is a cozy nest.

Although love grows,
within the feeling of sincere gratitude
and the warmth like feathers spreads throughout the body,
the trials that rush in like the shadow of fate
make the two wings flutter.

Enduring pain that feels like it could tear apart,
I sing the song of a free soul,
shouting it towards the blue sky.

날개

손등을 할퀼듯한 매서운 바람이 이는
절벽 끝자락
양지바른 곳에 아늑한 둥지가 있다

참으로 소중하고 고마운 감정 속에
사랑이 자라나고
깃털 같은 따스함이 온몸에 스며들어도
운명의 그림자처럼 밀려오는 시련은
두 날개를 퍼득이게 한다

찢어질 듯한 아픔을 참고
자유로운 영혼의 노래를 푸른 하늘 향해
목청껏 노래를 부르게 된다

The Swan Woman

At the swimming pool,
A woman
cuts through the water like a swan.
In a fine restaurant,
she dines elegantly like a peacock.

Flesh-colored band-aids are
stuck to her ankles and knees.

Through intense practice
and the pain of solitary training,
countless band-aids
have surely helped to create that graceful beauty.

백조의 여인

수영장에서
백조처럼 물을 가르던
한 여인
고급레스토랑에서 공작새처럼
우아한 모습으로 식사를 한다

발목과 무릎에
살색 반창고가 덕지덕지 붙어있다

혹독한 연습과
고독한 훈련의 괴로움 속에서
수많은 반창고가
저토록 아름다운 자태를 만들었으리라

Even in the Broken Pieces of a Jar

Carefully, one by one, I gathered them,
but only useless pieces remain.

On a hot summer day, like the heat of a kiln,
the fragments of forgotten memories
are carefully pieced together.

In a mosaic style more beautiful
than Byzantium,
it is reborn.

Within the broken pieces,
the soul of an old man who once made a pot alone
still breathes and lives.

깨진 항아리 조각에도

정성스레 한 점 한 점 모으다
쓸데없는 조각만 남았구나

가마 속 같이 더운 한여름날
잊히는 추억의 편린들
조심스럽게 조각들을 붙여 본다

비잔티움보다 더 아름다운
모자이크 항아리 양식으로
재탄생이 된다

깨진 조각 속에는
외롭게 독 짓던 한 늙은이의 혼이
아직도 살아 숨 쉬고 있다

The Children of the Monastery

With a clean-shaven head,
Dressed in a red robe,
A tender little novice monk,
Is he the child of the Buddha?

At the sound of the dawn bell,
His clear sound of reciting the scripture,
Like a chick under the shadow of the great monk,
Breaks through the sky.

In a tiny heart,
Dreaming of a white elephant,
He swells with great aspirations,
Blooming like the fresh green leaves of May.

Drawing his mother's image
With dew-like, sparkling eyes,
He awakens the dawn.

Child, you are the child of the Buddha,
With the virtue of compassion,
Grow and bloom with grace.

수도원의 아이들

파스르한 까까머리에
적삼 두른
여린 동자승
부처의 자식이런가?

새벽 타종에
큰스님 그늘에서
품어진 병아리 모습으로
경전 외는 맑은 소리가 창공을 뚫는다

자그만 가슴에
하얀 코끼리 꿈꾸며
큰 뜻을 품어
오월의 신록같이 부풀어 오르고 있다

엄마 모습 그리는
이슬 같은 영롱한 눈빛
새벽을 깨운다

동자야, 너는 부처의 자녀라
자비의 덕목으로
의젓이 피고 또 피어나라

A Tree with Deep Roots

On a hill where the wind howls,
There stands a life, lonely.

It wasn't by choice,
But unknowingly,
I was pushed here by the wind.

Inescapable fate,
I sank my roots and
Firmed the earth beneath me.

Though the storms come,
I remain strong,
Drawing strength from the light above,
And learning to love this place I stand.

With arms outstretched towards hope,
New leaves are shining
On the tightly woven rings of time.

뿌리 내린 나무

바람이 몰아치는 언덕 위
외롭게 서 있는
삶이 있다

좋아서가 아니고
나도 모르는 사이
바람에 등 떠밀려 이곳으로 왔다

어쩔 수 없는 숙명에
뿌리 내려
흙을 다져왔다

비바람 맞아도
하늘에서 내리는
찬란한 빛을 받으며
오늘 이곳을 사랑하게 되었다

희망을 향해 팔을 벌리고
촘촘한 나이테 위에
새로운 잎들이 반짝이고 있다

First Kiss

In a flower field glowing with golden light,
Two petals meet gently,
Reaching the limit with trembling body and heart.

Cheeks redder than poppies,
The swelling chest hides it all,
And softly, the eyes close.

In a moment where everything seems to stop,
Two pure figures,
In the thrill of a fleeting instant,
Promise eternity.

The most enchanting moment,
Unforgettable in life,
A fragment of the soul,
More beautiful than death.

첫 키스

황금빛이 발산되는 꽃밭
다소곳이 마주한 꽃잎들
파르르 떠는 몸과 마음의 임계치

양귀비꽃보다 더 붉은 두 뺨
부풀어 오르는 가슴에 묻고
살며시 눈을 감는다

모든 것이 멈춘 듯한
고결한 두 피사체
찰나의 짜릿함에
영원을 약속한다

삶에서 잊을 수 없는
가장 매혹적인 순간
죽음보다 아름다운
영혼의 한 조각

Stress Doesn't Exist

It's a big problem.
As the roof rises,
the pillar is too weak to hold it.

The young ones
squeeze their brains to find
a strong pillar,
while the older ones
adjust the roof to fit the pillar.

The two of them look at each other
and just laugh.

스트레스는 없다

큰일이다
지붕을 올리는데
기둥이 약해 버틸 수 없다

젊은이들은
큰 기둥을 구하기 위해
머리를 쥐어짜고
나이가 많이 든 사람은
기둥에 맞게 지붕을 올린다

두 사람은 서로 쳐다보고 웃기만 한다

The Scent of Chestnut Flowers

When I climb the mountain, a pungent smell fills the air.

It feels slightly dizzying and nauseating.

The red chatter that echoes
makes the early autumn leaves turn crimson.

밤꽃 향기

산에 오르면 비릿한 냄새가 진동한다

살짝 어지럽고 매쓰껍다

들려오는 빨간 재잘거림에
때 이른 단풍이 붉게 물든다

Waiting for Spring

The flowers that have reached the threshold of winter
no longer bloom.

Only the camellias, having endured the cold of the falling snow,
stain the white path with
their red petals.

In the blowing cold,
the clouds drift far away,
and the birds become silent.

As if left alone,
The season of contraction has arrived,
Felt in every part of me.

Through the frosted window,
my view trembles,
like leaves falling from trees.

When I open my heart in accordance with nature's order,
I see the spirits of spring walking toward me,
holding beautiful flowers in their chests,
coming closer to me.

봄을 기다리며

겨울의 문턱에 들어선 꽃들은
더 이상 피지 않습니다

눈 내리는 차가움을 견뎌낸 동백꽃만
붉은 꽃잎으로
하얀 길 위를 물들이고 있습니다

불어오는 추위에
구름은 멀리 달아나고
새들도 침묵에 듭니다

홀로 남겨진 듯
온몸으로 전해오는
위축의 계절이 되었습니다

서리 낀 창문 사이로
밖을 내다보는 시야가
나뭇잎 떨어지듯 흔들립니다

자연의 순리 따라 가슴을 열면
저만치 걸어오는 봄의 정령들
아름다운 꽃 가슴 가득히 안고
나에게 다가오고 있습니다

As the Year Comes to a Close

Joyful or regretful moments
are quietly drifting in my memories.

Like a faucet that can't be fully tightened,
emotions spill out uncontrollably.
If only they were like a rushing stream,
but another year passes by.

The echo of temple bells resonates softly,
like the gentle ripples in a lake.

With a calm heart, I send off the old year
and welcome the new one.
Regret and hope always cross paths.

한 해를 보내며

즐겁거나 아쉬운 일들
기억에서 혼연히 떠돌고 있습니다

잘 조절되지 않는 수도꼭지처럼
마구 새어 나오는 감정들
솟구치는 물줄기라면 좋았을 텐데
또 한 해가 지나갑니다

산사에서 울려오는 종소리의 여운
잔잔히 새겨지는 호수의 물결과도 같습니다

차분한 마음으로 보내고 맞이할
새해
아쉬움과 희망이 늘 교차하고 있습니다

Mystical Honey

My wife, whose stomach was unwell,
ate it first.

The pain in my ear
also healed.

Within the Manuka honey,
the staff of Asclepius was hidden.

신비한 꿀

위가 안 좋은 아내가
먼저 먹었다

아팠던
내 귀도 나았다

마누카꿀 속에
아스클레피오스의 지팡이가 숨어 있었다

Sending Off the Royal Chef

The late autumn of Bukjeong
always arrives with the cold winds of the valley.

At times, it brings with it
even the pain of parting.

Leaving behind the sorrow of a little chid,
with a motherly warmth turned away,
I step out,
treading on morning dew,
carrying the burden of a life as bitter as a sack of salt,
heading to the kitchen.

Like a royal chef who poured all her passion into guiding,
the daily dishes of kings unfold.
Following the royal chef's hands,
a feast of flavors blooms,
and in the overwhelming satisfaction,
the kitchen hums with happiness in all four seasons.

요리 상궁을 보내며

북정의 늦가을은
언제나 골짜기 찬바람을 데리고 나타납니다

때로는 아픈 이별까지
데리고 나타나기도 합니다

어린 핏줄의 설움을 그냥 둔 채
따스함을 뿌리친 모정으로
아침이슬 밟고
짜디짠 소금 자루 같은 삶을 걸머지고
주방으로 나옵니다

모든 열정 다 쏟아 지휘하던 상궁같이
날마다 펼쳐지는 왕들의 음식
영혼을 다 바친 상궁의 손길 따라
피어나는 맛의 향연
다물지 못하는 만족감에
요리궁은 사계절 행복함에 북적댑니다

As though sending off fragile siblings far away,
with a heart full of confusion and aching,
the hem of the worn-out apron
turns the corner of the earthen path.

In the lingering sorrow,
I stand there,
like a mindless basalt statue,
motionless, left behind.

가냘픈 오누이를 멀리 떠나보내듯
혼란스럽고 아린 심정에
낡은 행주치마 자락은
토담 길 모퉁이를 돌아서 갑니다

못내 아쉬움에
나는 정신 나간 현무암 석상처럼
그 자리에 덩그러니 서 있을 뿐입니다

The Great Doctor

With eyes that cannot see clearly ahead,
Can I look into the future?

Hoping for a more beautiful world to come,
I stood in a long line in front of the hospital.

Focused only on external matters, my vision is distorted,
All the pictures look askew, but
I must straighten the eye of my heart.

The heart that tries to halt the progression of macular degeneration,
Every word from the ophthalmologist
Draws all my attention

If there exists a great doctor
Who can heal both the body and the mind,
The steps I take on my way home
Will walk through a brighter world.

명의

앞이 잘 보이지 않는 눈으로
미래를 바라볼 수 있을까?

더 아름다운 세상이 오려나 기대하며
병원 앞에 길게 줄을 섰다

외적인 일에만 매달려 일그러진 시야
모든 그림이 비뚤비뚤하게 보이지만
마음의 눈만은 바로 잡아야겠다

황반변성의 진행을 막으려는 마음
안과 의사의 말 한마디마다
온 신경이 쏠린다

육체와 마음까지 고쳐 줄
명의가 있다면
집으로 돌아오는 발걸음이
더욱 환한 세상을 걸을 수 있겠지

Cellphone

Waking up to the sound of birds greeting me
With their beautiful voices,
I gently open the window.

Though it's a rather chilly autumn morning,
I send a warm greeting
to the people
who suddenly come to mind.

휴대폰

아름다운 목소리로 반기며
인사를 전하는 새소리에
잠에서 깨어나
살며시 창문을 열어봅니다

오늘 아침
제법 쌀쌀한 가을이지만
문득 떠오르는 사람들께
따스한 마음 담아
아침 인사를 전합니다

The Thinking Reed

Among countless stars,
Life lives
on the pale blue dot.

The many emptinesses
swaying in the wind
approach as if to swallow me whole.

Even if my thoughts are short,
I strive to understand the world.

I will fill the empty spaces of the universe
with love.

생각하는 갈대

수 많은 별 사이에
창백한 푸른 점에서
살고 있는 인생

바람에 흔들리는
많은 공허함이
나를 삼킬 듯 다가옵니다

생각이 짧다 해도
세상을 이해하려 애쓰고 있습니다

우주의 빈 곳을 사랑으로
채울 것입니다

On a Blank Sheet of Paper

I draw poetry.

I draw with a pure heart,
living in this beautiful world.

In the process of our consciousness
becoming flattened,
I also add the untold stories from the back alleys
and draw them.

Amid the rush of digital speed,
I also draw the forgotten pure values,
and unknown ideologies yet to be discovered.

I draw a small stream in front of the village,
flowing into the Milky Way,
as a fairytale story,
in the remaining blank space.

하얀 백지 위에

시를 그립니다

아름다운 세상에서 살고 있는
고운 마음을 넣어 그립니다

우리들의 의식이
평면화 되어 가는 과정에서
비추지 못한 뒷골목 이야기도 넣고
그려 봅니다

디지철 속도에 밀려 점점 잊혀 가는
순수한 가치나
아직 발굴되지 않은
미지의 이념도 그려 넣습니다

은하수로 흘러가는
마을 앞 실개천을
동화 같은 이야기로
남은 여백에 그려 넣습니다

Universal Values

A boat, tilted to the left,
is passing through the Han River.

The people on the right
are shooting arrows with their fingers,
causing the boat to rock.

Though I had long passed 17 years,
I still wanted to eat the dinner
my mother had prepared.

In the middle of the bridge,
I think:
Peace, friendship, and promises.
A feeling arose within me
that the boy must be saved.

보편적 가치

왼쪽으로 기울어진
한 척의 배가
한강을 지나가고 있다

오른쪽에 탄 사람들은
손가락으로 화살을 쏘며
배가 기우뚱거린다

17살을 훌쩍 건너가
어머니가 준비해주신
저녁을 먹고 싶었다

다리의 한 가운데에서
나는 생각한다
평화, 우정, 그리고 약속
소년을 반드시 구해야 한다는
마음이 들었다

Pioneering

Like a matchbox lit aflame,
the fortress crumbles, burning fiercely.
As if salt were poured into the Dead Sea,
the land of my homeland has become desolate.

Holding a child's hand,
with an old father carried on back,
the cold dew, like a mournful reed,
falls to the feet.

Thunder and lightning roar in the sky,
and on the sea, the high waves
make even the horizon disappear.

Carried in a boat, drifting like a buoy,
the lament of an exile who has lost his homeland.
"God, where are you sleeping?"

More beautiful than the sunset over the Aegean,
more passionate than the roses of Sicily,
I truly love
the brown-skinned women of Carthage.

개척

성냥갑에 불붙은 듯
활활 불타다 무너져내리는 성벽
사해에 소금을 뿌린 듯
황폐해져 버린 고국의 땅

어린아이 손 잡고
늙은 아비 등에 업으면
구슬픈 갈대에 맺힌 찬 이슬
발 등에 떨어진다

하늘에는 천둥 번개가 요란하고
바다에는 높은 파고에
수평선마저 보이지 않는다

나룻배에 몸을 싣고 부초 같이 떠다니는
고국 잃은 유랑자의 한탄
'신이여, 어디에 잠들어 계십니까?'

에게해의 노을빛보다 아름답고
시칠리아의 장미꽃보다 정열적인
카르타고의 갈색 여인들
진정으로 사랑합니다

Ah,
my beloved homeland,
from Asia, the dawn rises.

We are the red wolves of Troy,
in this vast land given by God,
on the green pasture,
we shall firmly build an eternal fortress.

아,
사랑하는 나의 모국
아시아로부터 먼동이 떠 오른다

우리는 트로이의 붉은 늑대들
광활한 이곳은 신이 주신 약속의 땅
푸른 초원 위에 영원한 성곽을 굳건히 세우렵니다

Consolation

In this lonely season when everything leaves,

Comfort and encouragement,
Though appreciated,
I would like to decline.

Because right now,
I am in the process of writing poetry.

위로

모든 것이 떠나가는 쓸쓸한 계절

위로와 격려는
고맙지만
사양하고 싶습니다

지금 나는
시詩를 쓰고 있는 중이기 때문입니다

Poetry

Opaque and unstable words,
gathered from here and there,
washed in clear spring water and neatly arranged,
then, my sincerity lingers there.

시詩

불투명하고 불안정한 언어들
이곳저곳에서 주워 모아
깨끗한 샘물에 헹구고 순서대로 정리하면
나의 진심이 벌써 그곳에 머문다

Poetry Creation

I am picking up pebbles by the riverbank.
The beautiful stones are not as easy to spot as I thought.
I manage to find one and carefully place it in my pocket.

A little while later, I find another beautiful stone.

I take it out of my pocket,
compare them both,
and coldly throw one away.
The creation of poetry continues.

시작詩作

강가에서 조약돌을 줍고 있습니다
생각보다 예쁜 돌이 눈에 안 띕니다
겨우 하나 주워 주머니 속에 고이 넣습니다

조금 뒤에 또 다른 예쁜 돌을 주었습니다

주머니에서 꺼내어
비교해 본 후
하나를 차갑게 던져 버립니다
시의 창작은 계속되고 있습니다

Song of Duino

In the west,
a long shadow of high sanctity is cast.
The ancient poet's fate,
unable to sleep to the sound of the reed pipe.

When I knock on the city gates,
the red sunset flows with the river,
in which many souls are reflected.

The guardian angel's hand feels distant,
while the sighs and unspoken cries of love
echo like a deer standing on a dead-end cliff,
its voice crying out in desperate despair.

From across the sea,
fear and loneliness blow,
yet the waking reed stands alone,
weaving the thread of poetry
with its sorrowful songs.

두이노의 노래

서쪽에 드리워진
높은 축성의 긴 그림자
풀피리 소리에 잠 못 들던
옛 시인의 숙명

성문을 두드리면
강물과 함께 흘러가는
붉은 노을에
수많은 영혼이 투영되어 보인다

수호천사의 구원의 손길은 요원하고
탄식과 못다한 사랑의 절규가
막다른 절벽 위에 서 있는 사슴처럼
목 놓아 울어대는 외침이 들린다

바다 저편에서 불어오는
두려움과 외로움도
홀로 참고 견뎌야 하는
깨어 있는 갈대의 구슬픈 노래가
시詩를 엮어내고 있다

【Epilogue】

Reading Jae Hyuk Lee's poetry collection "Three Prayers"
- The Inner Beauty Drawn from Experience -

Won Chul Choi
(Emeritus Professor at Pusan National University, Poet, Essayist)

Poetry is a sublimated art that sings of the essence of life.

It can take as its subject everything from living beings to inanimate nature, listening to the mysterious groan of the universe, contemplating oneself, or even possessing prophetic abilities to predict the future. These are the people who are poets.

Jae Hyuk Lee is a person with an engineering mindset and a natural talent in the arts. He particularly loves painting and has entered the world of poetry. He is currently managing Woori Farm. His home, which has no fence, is frequently visited by many neighbors, and he serves high-quality food to people. The entrance is always welcoming, with kindness and smiles greeting visitors.

Now, I am not writing a critique of Jae Hyuk Lee's second poetry collection *Three Prayers*. Rather than a critique, I want to speak about the journey he has been

【발문】

이제혁 시집 "세 번의 기도"를 읽고
- 체험에서 그려내는 내적 아름다움 -

최원철 (부산대명예교수, 시인, 수필가)

시詩는 삶의 근본을 노래하는 하나의 승화된 예술이다.

생명이 있는 것이나 없는 무생물의 자연까지 시詩의 대상을 삼기도 하고, 우주의 신비한 신음을 들으며 자신을 성찰하기도 하고 미래를 예측하는 예언적 능력을 가지기도 하는 자, 곧 그들이 시인이다.

이제혁 시인은 공학적인 사고를 가지고 있으며 예능적인 방면에도 소질을 가진 사람이다. 특히 그림 그리기를 좋아하면서 시詩의 세계에 뛰어들었다. 지금은 우리농원牛里農園을 경영하고 있다. 그의 집에는 울타리가 없이 많은 이웃들이 드나들며 질 좋은 음식을 사람들에게 대접하고 있다. 늘 친절함과 미소가 손님을 맞이하는 현관에 놓여있다.

지금, 필자가 이제혁 제2시집『세 번의 기도』를 읽고 시평을 하려고 하는 것이 아니다. 시평이라기 보다 발문으로 그의 지나온 일에 대해서 말하고 싶다. 그는 그의 고향인

through in this preface. He is a person who overcame many trials and hardships from his hometown of Cheongdo, Gyeongbuk, to settling in Yangsan, Gyeongnam. He seems to have a natural talent in both the arts and physical activities. He won swimming and wrestling competitions, was versatile in art, and eventually became a poet.

You can see fragments of his journey in his poetry as well. "Sitting alone on a cold bench in a foreign land with fallen leaves swirling around, I put a piece of bread in my mouth, but the yearning grows stronger, like hot tears falling from the leaves, the determination for success" (from *Tears Soaked Bread*).

Throughout his life, this poet has faced three major trials. Though he is not a religious person, he prayed for life. The first was a struggle with breathing difficulties on the highway, the second was a liver tumor, and the third prayer remains, a prayer for happiness. He transforms his true life struggles into poetry.

Jae Hyuk Lee is both generous and meticulous, not simply observing others' difficulties but helping them. He serves society and pursues happiness within his family. He is a poet who constantly reflects on his life and what true love and happiness are.

경북 청도에서 경남 양산에 자리 잡기까지 많은 시련과 고통을 이겨낸 사람이다. 특히 그는 예체능 방면에 타고난 소질을 가지고 있는 것 같다. 수영과 씨름대회에서 우승하는가 하면 미술에서도 다재다능하였고 심지어 시인으로써 우뚝 서게 되었다.

그가 지나온 일의 단편을 시(詩)에서도 볼 수 있다.

"이국땅에서 가랑잎 흩날리는 늦가을 싸늘한 벤치에 홀로 앉아 빵 조각 하나 입에 넣어봐도 울컥 고파지는 그리움, 나뭇잎처럼 뚝뚝 떨어지는 뜨거운 눈물, 성공의 결심" (눈물 젖은 빵 中)을 하게 된다.

이 시인이 살아오는 동안 세 번의 고통을 겪었다. 그는 신앙인이 아니지만 삶을 위한 기도를 올렸다. 첫 번째 고속도로에서 호흡곤란, 두 번째 그에게 찾아온 간(肝)의 종양, 세 번째 마지막 기도는 행복을 위한 기도가 아직 남아 있다. 고통에 대한 진정한 삶을 시(詩)로 승화시키고 있다.

이제혁 시인은 호탕하면서도 세심하고, 남의 어려움을 그냥 보기만 하지 않고 도와주며, 사회에 봉사와 가정의 행복을 추구하는 사람이다. 진정한 사랑과 행복이 무엇인가를 늘 가슴에 품고 자신을 성찰해 가는 시인이라고 생각한다.

Jae Hyuk Lee's poetry collection is divided into three parts: Part 1: A Joyful Journey Together, Part 2: Nest, Part 3: Even in the Broken Pieces of a Jar.

In **Part 1: A Joyful Journey Together,** he sings of life's journey in everyday life. He begins by speaking of the hardships he faced in his life's journey.

Breathlessness on the highway
standing suddenly at the threshold of life and death
I, with a desperate heart,
can only offer a silent prayer.
The hospital—just ten minutes away—
feels unbearably distant.

(omitted)

Two tumors in my liver,
a thunderbolt of news,
tension creeping in like an unshakable fear,
a wandering of regrets that keeps my eyes shut.

My body, unable to withstand
the passing of time.
Without a moment to say "I love you,"
my hands trembled alone.
A desperate prayer swirling in an empty heart.

이제혁 시집에 『제1부 함께하는 기쁜 여행』, 『제2부 둥지』, 『제3부 깨진 항아리 조각에도』등 세 부분으로 나누어져 있다.

『제1부 함께하는 기쁜 여행』에서는 생활 속 삶의 여정을 노래하고 있다. 먼저 작가의 삶의 여정에서 있었던 고통을 먼저 이야기하고 있다.

고속도로에서 일으킨 호흡곤란
갑작스런 생사의 문 앞에 선
나
애타는 마음에
간절한 기도뿐
10분 거리의 병원이 너무 멀었다

(중략)

간 속에 종양 두 개
날벼락 같은 소리에 무섭게 다가오는 긴장
눈을 뜰 수 없는 회한의 방황

흐르는 세월을 이겨내지 못한
나의 육신
사랑한다는 한마디 말 전할 겨를 없이
두 손만 떨릴 뿐
간절한 기도가 공전하는 공허한 마음

Both joy and hope were gone
and only fear remained to hold on to

Through tears flowing like a waterfall,
memories flashed like a passing lantern.
In my desperate heart,
wishing for just five more years,
two prayers rise and overwhelm me.

Finally,
a lifeline was thrown to rescue me from the swamp of anxiety.

Having been immersed in a peaceful life,
volunteering and hobbies
stitched meaning into my passing years.

Now, for myself,
I make three prayers
that will never truly end—

Saying the world has not yet ended.
                    - Excerpt from "Three Prayers"

In the poem above, the sudden onset of breathlessness occurs on the highway. In such an urgent situation, even though the hospital was only 10 minutes away,

기쁨도 희망도 잘려 나가고
두려운 마음만 붙들고 있을 때

폭포수같이 흐르는 눈물 속을
주마등처럼 스치는 추억
5년 만이라도 더 살 수 있도록
은총을 원하는 간절한 마음에
두 번의 기도가 나를 덮쳤다

드디어,
불안의 늪에서 구출될 생명줄이 던져졌다

평화로운 삶에 물들게 되어
봉사와 취미 생활이
지나온 세월의 역사(歷史)를
꾸미게 되었다

이제, 나를 위해
떼를 쓰며
끝낼 수 없는 세 번의 기도를 한다

세상이 아직 끝나지 않았다고
-「세 번의 기도」의 일부분

   위의 시에서 갑자기 찾아온 호흡곤란을 고속도로상에서 당한다. 정말 다급한 환경에서 병원이 10분 거리에 있어도

there was no time to spare, and the poet was overwhelmed. There was nothing but a desperate prayer. Then, once again, a liver tumor appeared, which was a thunderous shock to the poet. He could only raise his suffering with prayers, yet his heart was full of fear, as he couldn't bring himself to tell his wife and family the words "I love you." "joy and hope were gone / only fear remained to hold on to," the poet reflects. Amidst "Through tears flowing like a waterfall / memories flashed like a passing lantern", he prayed for "just five more years."

Since then, he has been living a "peaceful life," engaging in "volunteering and hobbies," while offering his third prayer, hoping to live well until the end of his life. This, in essence, is Jae Hyuk Lee's hope and a representation of his resilient spirit that overcomes despair.

Looking at Jae Hyuk Lee's poetry, one can see that his life's journey encompasses constant efforts both physically and mentally. Even though he grew up in a harmonious family, he has always pursued and forged his own path.

On the plane,
no matter how far I go,
it feels like an endless journey
through a foreign land.

당황하기 짝이 없었다. 오직 간절한 기도뿐이었다. 그리고 또다시 찾아온 간癌의 종양, 시인에게는 날벼락 같은 소리였다. 고통을 기도라는 투망으로 끌어올려 아내와 가족에게 사랑한다는 말 전하지 못한다는 두려운 마음이 앞서고 있었다. 그에게는 "기쁨도 희망도 잘려 나가고 / 두려운 마음만 붙들고", "폭포수같이 흐르는 눈물 속을 / 주마등처럼 스치는 추억"을 생각하며 "5년 만이라도 더 살 수 있도록" 해달라고 기도했다.

그후부터 지금까지 "평화로운 삶"으로 "봉사와 취미생활"을 하며 이 세상 끝날 때까지 잘 지낼 수 있도록 세 번째의 기도를 하고 있다. 이것이 이제혁 시인의 희망이며 절망을 이겨내는 단단한 그의 모습을 가진 셈이다.

이제혁 시인의 시편을 보면 삶의 여정에서 육체적으로나 정신적으로 끊임없는 노력을 내포하고 있다. 비록 화목한 가정에서 자랐을지라도 자신의 여정을 스스로 개척해 나가는 것을 알 수 있다.

**비행기에 올라
가도 가도 끝없는
이국의 고행길**

In the heart of a goose flying,
there is full of only loneliness.

Sitting alone on a cold bench
in a foreign land
with fallen leaves swirling around,

I put a piece of bread in my mouth,
but the yearning grows stronger.

Like hot tears falling
from the leaves,
The river flows with the determination for success
                - Full text of 「Tears-soaked Bread」

    In the first stanza above, the poet expresses the journey to a foreign land in search of a better life by saying, "On the plane / no matter how far I go / it feels like an endless journey / through a foreign land". However, upon leaving his homeland, a sense of loneliness arises in the poet's heart, which he expresses in the second stanza, saying, " In the heart of a goose flying / there is full of only loneliness."

    In the poet's work, terms such as "goose," "loneliness," "late autumn," "longing," and "leaves" are used to deepen the connection between autumn and loneliness.

    In the third stanza, "Sitting alone on a cold bench / in a foreign land / with fallen leaves swirling around / I put a piece of bread in my mouth / but the yearning grows

기러기 되어 날아가는 심정에
외로움만 가득하다
이국땅에서

가랑잎 흩날리는 늦가을
싸늘한 벤치에 홀로 앉아
빵 조각 하나 입에 넣어봐도
울컥 고파지는 그리움

나뭇잎처럼 뚝뚝 떨어지는
뜨거운 눈물
성공의 결심에 흐르는 강물

- 「눈물 젖은 빵」의 전문

 위의 첫 번째 연에 "비행기에 올라 / 가도 가도 끝없는 / 이국의 고행길" 작가의 더 좋은 삶을 위해 외국에 가는 것을 표현하고 있다. 막상 모국을 떠나고 보니 낯선 곳으로 가는 마음에는 외로움이 생겨 두 번째 연에서 "기러기 되어 날아가는 심정에 / 외로움만 가득하다"고 말하고 있다.
 시인의 시편에서 "기러기", "외로움", "늦가을", "그리움", "나뭇잎", 등을 이용한 시어들을 나열하여 가을과 외로움의 관계를 짙게 나타내고 있다.
 세 번째 연에서 "이국땅에서 / 가랑잎 흩날리는 늦가을 / 싸늘한 벤치에 홀로 앉아 / 빵 조각 하나 입에 넣어봐도 / 울컥 고파지는 그리움"이 시인의 처지를 잘 나타내고 있다. 아는 이

stronger," the poet's situation is well captured. Sitting alone on a cold bench in a foreign land, with no familiar faces around, during the bleak late autumn, how much must the poet have missed his family and friends from home? Rather than saying that tears poured out from the loneliness, the poet describes how the longing grew, which highlights the depth of his homesickness.

Furthermore, in the last fourth stanza, in the state of loneliness and longing, "Like hot tears falling / from the leaves," the poet expresses his determination to succeed in this foreign land by saying, "The river flows with the determination for success".

Writing this preface, I too, as I read *Tears-soaked Bread*, recall the time in the 1970s when I was studying for my doctorate in Germany, and the memories pass through my mind like a flash. Who hasn't shed tears for the success of the future? Now, it seems that Jae Hyuk Lee must have deeply longed for his homeland during that time. He must have stayed up through many lonely nights.

In **Part 2: Nest,** the focus is primarily on family, and I would like to first introduce a poem that expresses the author's heart.

아무도 없는 외로운 이국 땅에서 더더구나 스산한 늦가을에 홀로 벤치에 앉아 배고파 빵한 조각을 입에 넣을 때 얼마나 고향의 가족이나 친지들이 보고 싶지 않았을까? 쓸쓸한 마음에 눈물이 왈칵 쏟아진다고 하지 않고 오히려 시인은 그리움이 고파진다고 하였다.

뿐만 아니라 마지막 네 번째 연에서 외롭고 그리운 상태에서 "나뭇잎처럼 뚝뚝 떨어지는/ 뜨거운 눈물"은 이국에서 열심히 일을 하여 성공을 해야겠다는 의지를 시인은 "성공의 결심에 흐르는 강물"로 표현하고 있다.

발문을 쓰고 있는 나 자신도 「눈물 젖은 빵」을 읽어 볼 때 1970년대에 독일에서 박사학위 공부하던 때가 주마등같이 뇌리를 스치고 지나가고 있다. 앞날의 성공을 위해 눈물 흘리지 않는 사람이 어디 있겠는가? 이제혁 시인은 그 당시 참담하도록 모국이 그리워 졌을 것이다. 밤마다 외로움으로 하얗게 지새웠을 것이다.

『제2부 둥지』에서 주로 가정을 노래하고 있는데 먼저 자신의 마음을 나타낸 시편을 소개하고자 한다.

When my mind becomes complicated,
sometimes,
I go to the reservoir
and fish.

The familiar people
place several fishing rods
and wait for the fish.

I, waiting on a single line,
pour all my attention into the fishing.

Rather than living entangled
in complexity,
it is more joyful to live simply.

I cast my love on the single line,
and with a focused gaze,
I look at one place,
my heart, red and pure

                  - The full text of 「Single-Line Fishing」

  In *Part 2: Nest*, Jae Hyuk Lee expresses his feelings in the poem "Single Line Fishing." "When my mind becomes complicated / sometimes / I go to the reservoir /
and fish." While some people place several fishing rods / and wait for the fish," the poet says "I, waiting

마음이 복잡해질 때
가끔,
저수지에 가서
낚시를 한다

익숙한 사람들은
여러 개의 낚싯대를 놓고
물고기를 기다린다

하나의 낚싯대에 매달려 기다리는
나
외줄낚시에 온 정성을 기울인다

복잡하게
얽히고설키면서
살아가는 것보다
단순하게 살아가는 것이 즐겁다

외줄낚시에 사랑을 드리우고
오롯이 한 곳을 바라보는
붉은 내 마음

        - 「외줄낚시」의 전문

  이제혁 시인은 『제2부 둥지』에서 자신의 마음을 「외 줄낚시」에서 표현하고 있다. "마음이 복잡해질 때 / 가끔, / 저수지에 가서 / 낚시를 한다". 어떤 이들은 "여러 개의 낚싯

on a single line / pour all my attention into the fishing." He continues, "Rather than living entangled / in complexity / it is more joyful to live simply." In the final stanza, he writes, "I cast my love on the single line / and with a focused gaze / I look at one place / my heart, red and pure." This shows his upright and sincere heart. Despite living in a chaotic generation, I believe that readers can deeply resonate with this poem.

Jae Hyuk Lee also expresses his deep affection for his hometown in poems such as *"A Quiet Countryside Sketch," "My Wife's Footsteps," "Scent of My Father,"* and especially *"Badminton Story," "To My Son,"* and *"Daughter's Birthday."* In these works, the poet honestly conveys his heartfelt emotions towards his children. His expressions of love for his family are sung in *"Nest."*

With a heart full of excitement, I gently hold your hand, and unknowingly, I see the calluses formed over time, the traces of the years embedded within.

In the secret garden we walk through, yellow lilacs bloom beautifully.

When we turn our steps back toward the rear garden,

대를 놓고 / 물고기를 기다"리고 있으나 이 시인은 "하나의 낚싯대에 매달려" "온 정성을 기울인다"고 하며 "복잡하게 얽히고설키면서 / 살아가는 것보다 / 단순하게 살아가는 것이 즐겁다"고 하며 마지막 연에서 "외줄낚시에 사랑을 드리우고 / 오롯이 한 곳을 바라보는 / 붉은 내 마음"이라고 자신의 올곧은 마음을 나타내고 있다. 이러한 마음을 아무리 질서 없는 세대에서 살아가는 사람들이라도 독자들이 충분히 공감할 수 있는 시편이라고 생각한다.

   이제혁 시인은 고향을 나타내는 「고즈넉한 시골의 소묘」와 「아내의 발자국」, 「아버지의 향내」, 특히 「베드민턴 이야기」, 「아들에게」, 「딸아이의 생일」에는 작가의 자녀에 대한 애틋한 마음을 솔직하게 말하고 있다. 시인이 가지고 있는 가정에 대한 사랑의 표현을 「둥지」에서 노래하고 있다.

설레는 마음으로 살며시 잡은 손
나도 몰래 굳은살 알알이 박여있는
세월의 흔적을 들여다본다

함께 거니는 비원祕苑에는
노란 라일락이
예쁘게 피어나고 있다

다정히 걸어가는 발걸음을
후원後苑으로 돌렸을 때

five crimson roses
bloom gracefully.

On the distant ridges of the mountains,
cherry blossoms and nightingales sing,
and with joy in my heart,
I walk and walk, toward the season ahead.

-The full text of 「Nest」 -

In the poem above, the poet takes his wife's hand, something he had forgotten to do over the years. In her hand, he discovers "the calluses formed over time, the traces of the years embedded within." revealing both his regret and gratitude.

Now, as he looks around the garden (symbolizing family), he sees his children blooming beautifully like happy flowers. He expresses his joy, envisioning a future where "On the distant ridges of the mountains / cherry blossoms and nightingales sing / and with joy in my heart / I walk and walk, toward the season ahead."

Part 3: Even in the Broken Pieces of a Jar

In *Humans on Earth*, poet Jae Hyuk Lee reflects on humanity's journey in search of a better life, tracing its origins back to Africa and Mesopotamia. He also

담홍빛 장미 5송이
우아하게 피어나고

멀리 보이는 산등성이에
산벚꽃도 소쩍새도 노래하는 계절을 향해
환희에 찬 걸음을 걷고 걷는다
　　　　　　　　　　　　- 「둥지」의 전문

　위의 시詩에서 시인은 지금까지 살아오며 잊고 있었던 아내의 손을 잡아본다. 아내의 손에서 발견한 것은 "나도 몰래 굳은살 알알이 박여있는 / 세월의 흔적을 들여다본다"고 미안함과 고마운 마음을 동시에 가지고 있는 것을 알 수 있다.
　이제 정원(가정)을 살펴보면 자식들이 행복한 꽃들로 예쁘게 피어나고 미래의 "산등성이에 / 산벚꽃도 소쩍새도 노래하는 계절을 향해 / 환희에 찬 걸음을 걷고 걷는다"고 행복을 토로하고 있다.

『제3부 깨진 항아리 조각에도』

　이제혁 시인은 「지구상의 인간들」에서 인류가 좀 더 나은 삶을 위해 찾아 나선 발자취의 기점을 아프리카와 메소포타미아에서 나간 것에 의미를 두고 우리나라의 건국 기원

incorporates mythical narratives related to the founding of Korea. In *Wings*, he sings of the freedom of the soul.

Human existence is inherently unstable. No matter how much civilization advances or culture flourishes, humans cannot attain eternity. Even with scientific progress, we remain bound by limited time and finite matter. In *Even in the Broken Pieces of a Jar*, the poet contemplates the journey of life from this perspective.

Carefully, one by one, I gathered them,
but only useless pieces remain.

On a hot summer day, like the heat of a kiln,
the fragments of forgotten memories
are carefully pieced together.

In a mosaic style more beautiful
than Byzantium,
it is reborn.

Within the broken pieces,
the soul of an old man who once made a pot alone
still breathes and lives.
 - Full Text of 「Even in the Broken Pieces of a Jar」

In the poem above, the poet is seen piecing together the fragments of a precious jar that was once whole. It is unclear whether the jar was inherited from his

에 대한 신화적 이야기를 하고 있다. 그리고 「날개」에서는 자유로운 영혼의 노래를 부른다.

　인간은 매우 불안정하다. 문명이 눈부시게 발달하고 문화가 아무리 발전해도 인간은 영원할 수가 없다. 과학이 발달해도 제한된 시간과 제한된 물질로 된 인간을 벗어날 수 없다. 「깨진 항아리 조각에도」에 시인이 내다보는 삶의 여정을 나타내고 있다

**정성스레 한 점 한 점 모으다
쓸데없는 조각만 남았구나**

**가마 속 같이 더운 한여름날
잊히는 추억의 편린들
조심스럽게 조각들을 붙여 본다**

**비잔티움보다 더 아름다운
모자이크 항아리 양식으로
재탄생이 된다**

**깨진 조각 속에는
외롭게 독 짓던 한 늙은이의 혼이
아직도 살아 숨 쉬고 있다**
　　　　　　　　　- 「깨진 항아리 조각에도」의 전문

　위의 시詩에서 시인이 귀한 항아리를 가지고 있다가 깨어진 조각들을 맞추고 있는 것이다. 그 항아리가 부모로 부

parents or simply something of great value. However, as he carefully assembles the broken pieces, he senses the spirit of an old potter who once worked in solitude, breathing life into the fragments.

These shards may also symbolize his own scattered memories, shattered and dispersed over time, which he now attempts to gather and reconstruct. Although the jar is restored to its shape, it is no longer as perfect as it once was. Yet, rather than lament its imperfections, the poet envisions the reassembled jar as a mosaic more beautiful than a Byzantine vessel, expressing the idea that the soul of the artisan still lingers within the broken pieces.

In particular, poet Jae Hyuk Lee, in *"A Tree with Deep Roots,"* reflects in the first stanza on how his early life was intertwined with loneliness, much like a tree standing alone on a wind-swept hill.

On a hill where the wind howls,
There stands a life, lonely.

It wasn't by choice,
But unknowingly,
I was pushed here by the wind.

터 물려받은 것인지, 매우 귀중한 것인지를 알 수 없지만 그 조각들 속에 외롭게 독 짓던 늙은이의 혼이 스며 있는 것을 느끼며 조각들을 붙이고 있는 것이다. 그 조각들이 한 편 자신이 지나온 추억들이 산산이 흩어진 것을 회상하며 편린들을 모으고 있었을 것이다. 비록 조각들을 맞추어 내어 항아리 모양이 복구되었지만, 처음같이 완전하지는 않았을 것이다. 그러나 시인은 그 조각들을 비잔티움의 항아리보다 더 아름다운 모자이크 항아리로 보았고 깨어진 조각들 장인의 혼이 숨 쉬고 있음을 표현하고 있다.

특히 이재혁 시인은 「뿌리 내린 나무」에서 그의 조기의 삶은 바람이 몰아치는 언덕 위에 외로움과 연결되어 있음을 제1연에서 회상하고 있다.

바람이 몰아치는 언덕 위
외롭게 서 있는
삶이 있다

좋아서가 아니고
나도 모르는 사이
바람에 등 떠밀려 이곳으로 왔다

Inescapable fate,
I sank my roots and
firmed the earth beneath me.

Though the storms come,
I remain strong,
Drawing strength from the light above,
And learning to love this place I stand.

With arms outstretched towards hope,
New leaves are shining
On the tightly woven rings of time.
Full Text of 「A Tree with Deep Roots」

In the second stanza, the poet writes, "It wasn't by choice / But unknowingly / I was pushed here by the wind." This likely refers to Yangsan, the place where he has now settled and built his life. Thus, in the third stanza, he expresses, "Inescapable fate / I sank my roots and / firmed the earth beneath me."

I sometimes visit the 'Woori Farm,' where poet Jae Hyuk Lee has settled. There are no fences here. The spacious parking lot is filled with visitors' cars, and at the poet's doorstep, the warm smiles of the poet and his wife are always there to welcome guests.

In the fourth stanza, the poet says, "Though the storms come / I remain strong / Drawing strength from

어쩔 수 없는 숙명에
뿌리내려
흙을 다져왔다

비바람 맞아도
하늘에서 내리는
찬란한 빛을 받으며
오늘 이곳을 사랑하게 되었다

희망을 향해 팔을 벌리고
촘촘한 나이테 위에
새로운 잎들이 반짝이고 있다

「뿌리 내린 나무」의 전문

   제2연에서 "좋아서가 아니고 / 나도 모르는 사이 / 바람에 등 떠밀려 이곳으로 왔다" 이곳은 현재 터전을 잡고 살고 있는 양산을 이야기하고 있을 것이다.
   나는 가끔 이제혁 시인이 터를 잡고 있는 '우리牛里농원'에 들린다. 이곳에는 울타리가 없다. 넓은 주차장에 꽉 차 있는 손님의 자동차들, 시인의 현관에는 시인과 시인의 아내의 미소가 항상 기다리고 있다.
   제4연에서 시인이 때로는 "비바람 맞아도 / 하늘에서 내리는 / 찬란한 빛을 받으며 / 오늘 이곳을 사랑하게 되었다"

the light above / And learning to love this place I stand." This place has become his second hometown, where he wholeheartedly welcomes guests while diligently writing poetry amid his busy life. He is a poet who truly understands life, for his life itself is poetry.

In the final fifth stanza, it is evident that as he continues to live, he strives toward hope. He confesses, "With arms outstretched towards hope / New leaves are shining / On the tightly woven rings of time.." Truly, poet Jae Hyuk Lee is living a meaningful and valuable life.

Living far from the intersection of poetry and lyricism in life may be considered unfortunate. We believe that having the creativity, cognitive abilities, and insight to exist within such a poetic environment enriches life and gives it profound meaning.

In the journey of life, faced with sudden physical danger, the poet begins his second collection with prayer, opening up a new genre. He transforms the inner beauty drawn from experience into poetry.

There is still the third prayer remaining for poet Jae Hyuk Lee.

For his third prayer, we hope he becomes a poet who can hear the higher cosmic breath and groans, singing the absolute values and eternity of life. Poetry is a means of life, not its purpose, so he must become a true poet who can communicate with the pure and

제2의 고향이 되어 온 정성을 다하여 손님을 대하며 바쁜 가운데 시_詩를 쓰고 있는 것이다. 진정한 삶을 아는 시인인 것이다. 그의 삶이 곧 시_詩이기 때문이다.

마지막 제5연에서 그는 살아갈수록 희망을 향해 매진하고 있음을 알 수 있다. 즉, "희망을 향해 팔을 벌리고 / 촘촘한 나이테 위에 / 새로운 잎들이 반짝이고 있다"고 고백하고 있다. 참으로 이제혁 시인은 값진 삶을 살고 있다.

삶 속의 시_詩와 서정의 교차점에서 멀리 떨어져 사는 것이 불행일지 모른다. 우리는 이러한 시적 환경 속에서 살 수 있는 창의성이나 인지능력으로 통찰력을 가져야 함이 삶을 윤택하고 매우 의미 있는 일이라 생각한다.

삶의 여정에서 갑작스럽게 다가온 육체적인 위험에서 기도로부터 시작한 제2시집의 새로운 장르를 펼치고 있다. 체험에서 그려내는 내적 아름다움을 시_詩로 승화시키고 있다.

이제혁 시인에게는 아직 세 번째의 기도가 남아 있다.

세 번째의 기도를 위해 삶의 절대적 가치와 영원을 노래하는 차원 높은 우주의 숨소리나 신음을 들을 수 있는 시인이 되기를 바란다. 시는 삶의 수단이지만 목적이 아니기 때문에 순결하고 고결한 영혼의 세계와 서로 교통할 수 있는 시인으로 죽음까지 벗어버릴 수 있는 참다운 시인이 되어야 할

noble world of the soul and transcend even death. Since his third prayer remains, he is an incredibly fortunate poet. We hope that, in the future, he becomes a poet admired and respected by all.

것이다. 아직 세 번째의 기도가 남아있으니 얼마나 행복한 시인인 줄 모른다. 앞으로 누구나 부러워하고 존경받는 시인이 되기를 한 번 더 빌어본다.

미산(彌山) 이 제 혁
Sumeru, Jae Hyuk LEE

\<시인\>
우리농원 대표

\<Poet\>
Representative of Woori Farm

Debuted in the New Poet Association of New Busan on November 30, 2022
Member of the Poet Association of New Busan
Member of the Busan Writers' Association
Member of the Cheonseong Writers' Association
Member of the Poet Society of Yang San

세 번의 기도
Three Prayers 정가 20,000원

2025년 5월 16일 인쇄
2025년 5월 20일 발행

저 자 : 이 제 혁
발행인 : 박 중 열
발행처 : 다솜출판사
인쇄처 : 효성문화사

등록번호 : 1994년 4월 22일 제325-2001-000001호
부산광역시 중구 대청로 135번길 10-1
TEL : (051)462-7207 / 8 FAX : (051)465-0646

ISBN 978-89-5562-814-2 03810

이 책의 무단복제를 금함.